The Nine Planets

EXPLORING OUR UNIVERSE

The Nine Planets

REVISED EDITION

by Franklyn M. Branley

Illustrated by Helmut K. Wimmer

THOMAS Y. CROWELL COMPANY

NEW YORK

BY THE AUTHOR:
Experiments in the Principles of Space Travel
Solar Energy
Exploring by Satellite: The Story of Project Vanguard
Experiments in Sky Watching
Man in Space to the Moon

Exploring Our Universe
The Nine Planets
The Moon: Earth's Natural Satellite
Mars: Planet Number Four
The Sun: Star Number One
The Earth: Planet Number Three
The Milky Way: Galaxy Number One

To Millie C. Lemon

Contents

THE FAMILY OF PLANETS

THE EARTH IS A PLANET. It is a member of the family of nine planets that revolve around the sun, the center of our solar system. Because the earth is our home we, of course, feel that the earth is the most important and the most interesting of all the planets. But the other planets are interesting too; some of them are much larger than the earth, some of them smaller, or hotter, or colder. Each is different. The ancients called them wandering stars because they seem to wander—to change position against the background of stars.

Named in order of distance from the sun, the planets are: Mercury, Venus, Earth, Mars, Jupiter, Saturn, Uranus, Neptune, and Pluto. The distances of the planets from the sun are shown in the table.

Planet	Symbol	Distance (Miles)
MERCURY	☿	36,000,000
VENUS	♀	67,200,000
EARTH	⊕	92,900,000
MARS	♂	141,500,000
JUPITER	♃	483,300,000
SATURN	♄	886,000,000
URANUS	♅	1,783,000,000
NEPTUNE	♆	2,791,000,000
PLUTO	♇	3,664,000,000

If you were making a model of the solar system, you could start by placing Mercury 1 inch from the sun. Then Venus would be 1⅔ inches from the sun; Earth, 2½ inches; Mars, just under 4 inches; Jupiter, about 13¼ inches; Saturn, about 24½ inches; Uranus, a little over 4 feet; Neptune, about 6½ feet; and Pluto, 8½ feet.

A model out of doors could be made on a larger scale. About a hundred years ago Sir John Herschel developed a scale that went like this. If the earth were the size of a pea, then Mercury would be 82 feet from the sun, Venus 142 feet, Earth 215 feet, Mars 327 feet, Jupiter 1320 feet, Saturn 2112 feet, Uranus 3960 feet (¾ mile), Neptune 6600 feet (1¼ miles). Pluto would be 8580 feet away (1⅝ miles).

You would need a big field to make this model. Sir John did not expect anyone really to make it. He merely suggested the

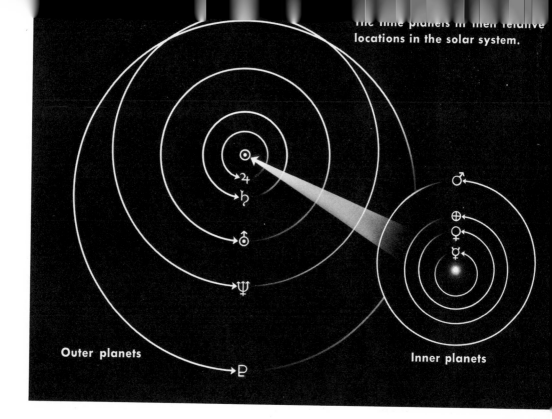

Outer planets

Inner planets

model to help us understand how large our system of planets really is.

The distances of the planets from the sun fall into a pattern. The pattern, or relationship, was made popular in the eighteenth century by Johann Elert Bode, a German mathematician-astronomer. Bode, and other astronomers such as Titius of Wittenberg, had observed the distances of the planets from the sun. They wondered whether there was any relationship among the distances or whether the planets were, instead, located at random. After carefully noting the distances and after long and painstaking effort, Titius, who was also a mathematician, found a relationship. But even though Titius discovered it, the formula became known as Bode's Law—because Bode made it popular.

To understand Bode's Law (which is really a relationship and not a law), you must know what is meant by the astronomical unit. Just as you and I use the mile as a unit to measure distances, so astronomers use the mean distance from the sun to the earth (92,900,000 miles) as the astronomical unit.

You may wonder what mean distance is. This is the way it is determined. The distance between the sun and the earth varies at different places in the orbit. The greatest distance is some 3 million miles more than the least. This is because the earth's orbit is an ellipse—as are the orbits of all the planets. The sun is not at the center, but at a location called the focus; and so the distance from a planet to the sun varies. To get the mean distance, we determine the distance between the planet and the sun at various times and tabulate these measurements in order, from the shortest to the longest. The figure that is midway between the longest and shortest is the mean distance. This is not the same as the average figure. For example, the mean of these figures is 10 because it is midway between 2 and 16.

$$2 - 4 - 6 - 7 - \mathbf{10} - 12 - 13 - 14 - 16$$

Bode's Law works like this. Write out the numbers 0, 3, 6, 12, 24, and so on, each time doubling the next number, until you reach 768; then add 4 to each number. The results will be ten times the distances between the planets and the sun in astronomical units (A.U.). For example:

Mercury	Venus	Earth	Mars	Asteroids
0	3	6	12	24
4	4	4	4	4
4	7	10	16	28
0.4	0.7	1.0	1.6	2.8

Jupiter	Saturn	Uranus	Neptune	Pluto
48	96	192	384	768
4	4	4	4	4
52	100	196	388	772
5.2	10.0	19.6	38.8	77.2

The first figure is the distance from the sun to Mercury: 0.4 astronomical units, or about 37,160,000 miles. The 38.8, for instance, means that Neptune should be about that many astronomical units from the sun—or about 3,604,520,000 miles.

Planet	Actual Distance (A.U.)	Distance According to Bode's Law (A.U.)
MERCURY	0.39	0.40
VENUS	0.72	0.70
EARTH	1.00	1.00
MARS	1.52	1.60
JUPITER	5.20	5.20
SATURN	9.54	10.00
URANUS	19.18	19.60
NEPTUNE	30.06	38.80
PLUTO	39.52	77.20

The table shows that the actual distances to the planets, in astronomical units, agree quite well with the distances predicted by Bode's Law. This surely is true for all the planets except Neptune and Pluto. Maybe Bode's Law applies only to certain planets. So far as we know, there is no scientific reason why it should apply at all. Perhaps it is just a coincidence that parts of it correspond so closely to actual measurements.

But even if it is a coincidence, the relationship helped astronomers to find the asteroids, or minor planets. If you look at the table of distances on page 4, you will see a column labeled "Asteroids," and a distance of 2.8 A.U. indicated. There was found to be a gap between Mars and Jupiter—and so astronomers looked for something in that gap. Their searching led to the discovery of the first asteroid on January 1, 1801. It was named Ceres after the Romans' goddess of vegetation, who was closely related to their earth goddess.

Since 1801 many other asteroids have been discovered. Astronomers believe there are tens of thousands—perhaps as many as 50,000—that we have not yet located.

Ceres, the largest asteroid, has a diameter of some 450 miles. All the planets are much larger than the largest asteroid. However, the planets vary greatly in size. Some planets are much smaller than the earth, some much larger. The smaller ones are called terrestrial (earthlike) planets. They are Mercury, Venus, Earth, Mars, and Pluto. The major planets are Jupiter, Saturn, Uranus, and Neptune. Frozen gases make up a large part of the total size of the major planets. The particles of gases in the atmospheres of all the major planets are closely packed. The particles in the atmospheres of the minor planets are spread out more thinly.

The smallest planet is Mercury; the largest is Jupiter. Jupiter is so large that its diameter is almost thirty times greater than the diameter of Mercury.

If you were to make models of the planets to a usable scale—that is, a scale that will not make the small planets too small, nor the large planets too large—you could use a scale of 8000 miles to an inch. On this scale the planets would have the following diameters: Mercury, a little less than ½ inch; Venus, just under 1 inch; Earth, just a bit larger than Venus; Mars, ½ inch;

Jupiter, just about 11 inches; Saturn, just under 9 inches; Uranus, just over 3½ inches; Neptune, 3¼ inches; and Pluto, just under ½ inch.

Planet	Mean Diameter (Miles)
MERCURY	3,100
VENUS	7,700
EARTH	7,918
MARS	4,200
JUPITER	88,700
SATURN	75,100
URANUS	29,500
NEPTUNE	27,700
PLUTO	3,600 (?)

Sir John Herschel worked out the following scale for the planets. He said that Mercury should be represented by a mustard seed, Venus a pea, Earth a pea also, Mars a large pinhead, Jupiter an orange, Saturn a small orange, Uranus a cherry and Neptune a good-sized plum. Pluto should be a small pea.

Symbols of the Planets

Each planet has a symbol, derived from a god or goddess with whom the planet was associated. The reason for each symbol goes back to ancient mythology.

Mercury (☿) is derived from a wand with two serpents wound about it. This wand, called the caduceus, was carried by the god Hermes, or Mercury.

Venus (♀) is a hand mirror. Venus is the goddess of love and beauty, so a hand mirror is altogether proper.

Mars is named after the god of war, perhaps because of its

blood-red color. A shield and spear are the symbol for Mars (♂).

The ancients named Jupiter after the king of the Roman gods. Although the name is from the Roman god, the symbol (♃) is taken from Zeus, the king of the Greek gods; the symbol is a great thunderbolt, or the letter Z.

Saturn was named after the god of time because the planet moved so slowly among the stars. The symbol (♄) of the planet is a sickle, which reminds one of the scythe carried by Father Time.

The symbol for Uranus (♅) represents the heavens: Uranus was the Greek god of the skies. As god of the skies he supplied the earth with the warmth of the sun and the moisture of rain. Uranus is shown frequently as an old, bearded man holding a robe stretched above his head to form an arch.

Neptune was the Roman god of the sea. The planet is represented by a three-pointed fork, the trident of Father Neptune (♆). The Romans used to have festivals to Neptune in mid-July, when lakes and streams were drying up, in the hope that he would fill them once more.

The ancients did not realize that the earth is a planet, and they did not know of Uranus, Neptune, and Pluto because these three planets cannot be seen without the aid of a telescope. Therefore the symbols for the earth and the last three planets are modern. The symbol (⊕), which represents the earth, shows the equator and a line passing from the North Pole to the South Pole.

Pluto was discovered in 1930. The symbol for it (♇) is made from the two letters P and L, which stand for Percival Lowell, the person who did much of the work that led to the discovery of Pluto by Clyde Tombaugh. Over a long period of time Lowell (and other men) observed slight changes in the motion of Neptune. He demonstrated mathematically that these changes were

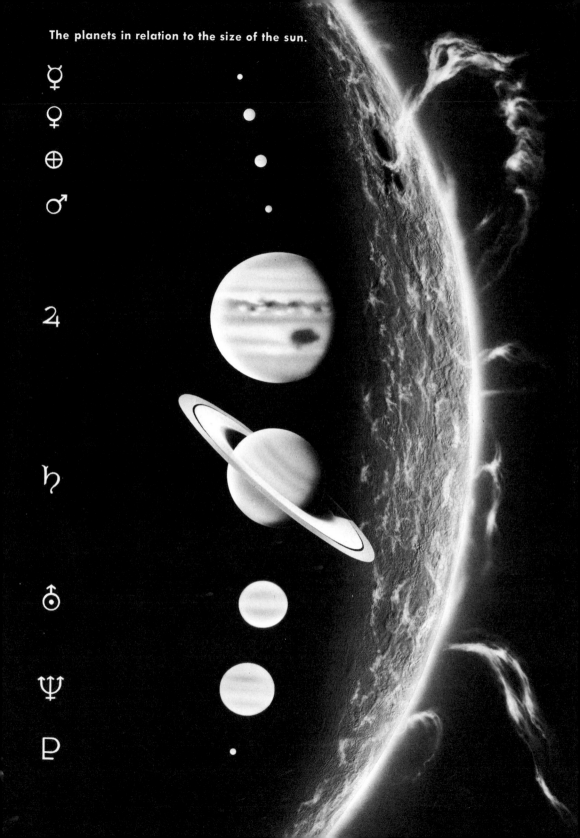

The planets in relation to the size of the sun.

caused by an object, probably a planet, that was close by. Lowell predicted in what area of the sky the new planet would be found, but he died before the discovery was made.

Density of the Planets

In astronomy a planet is described by its density, mass, volume, and so on. Density tells us how closely the parts that make up something are packed together. For instance, we give water a density of 1, and then measure the densities of other substances as they compare with water. If the atoms of another material are packed closer together, its density is greater than 1. A pint of water weighs 1 pound; and water has a density of 1. Suppose we find that a pint of some other material weighs 2 pounds. This implies that the atoms are packed closer together. This material would have a density of 2.

The density of the earth is 5.52. This means that if we mixed together all the water, atmosphere, and solids of the earth and then took a pint of that mixture, it would weigh 5.52 pounds— or 5.52 times the weight of a pint of water, which is 1 pound.

The densities of the other planets are shown in the table.

Planet	Density (Water = 1)
MERCURY	5.13
VENUS	4.97
EARTH	5.52
MARS	3.96
JUPITER	1.34
SATURN	0.69
URANUS	1.56
NEPTUNE	2.27
PLUTO	4.00 (?)

Notice that the minor planets are more dense than the major planets. Saturn has the lowest density. In fact, its density is so low that Saturn would float on water, if we could find a lake large enough to put it into. All the other planets, including the earth, would sink in this imaginary lake because they have densities greater than 1.

Mass of the Planets

Mass tells us how much material—air, water, and solids all together—is contained in a planet. Mass gives information about the relative number of molecules contained in a substance—as distinguished from weight, which is a measure of gravitational attraction. If you should move to the moon, where the gravity is one sixth that of the earth, your weight would be one sixth your earth weight—but your mass would still be the same. Suppose we say that the mass of the earth is 1; then Mars will have a mass of 0.107. This means that Mars contains 0.107 times as much material as the earth contains.

The masses of the other planets are shown in the table.

Planet	Mass (Earth = 1)
MERCURY	0.056
VENUS	0.814
EARTH	1.000
MARS	0.107
JUPITER	318.000
SATURN	95.200
URANUS	14.600
NEPTUNE	17.300
PLUTO	?

For the mass of a planet to be computed, the planet must be observed over a long period of time to determine how much its gravitational attraction causes other planets to vary from the positions predicted for them. We have been watching Pluto only since 1930. In that time it has gone only about one eighth of the way around its orbit, and we have not been able to gather sufficient information about its effect on other planets to figure out its mass precisely. However, it may be about the same as the mass of the earth—probably a bit smaller.

Inclination of the Orbits

The orbits of the planets, including the earth, are on essentially the same plane. They vary a little from a perfectly flat plane; but none of them varies very much except Pluto.

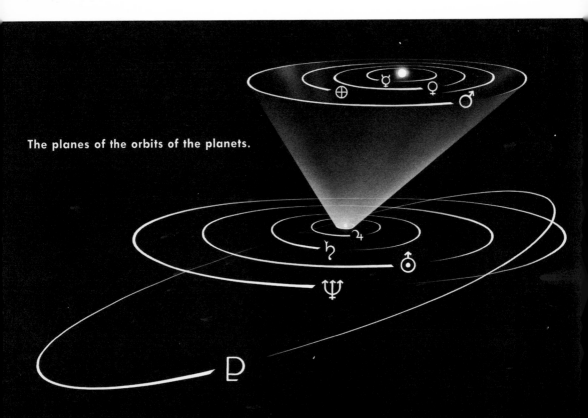

The planes of the orbits of the planets.

The upper part of the illustration here shows the inner orbits, and we see below it how these fit into the over-all arrangement of the solar system. The orbit of Pluto is tilted 17 degrees from the earth's orbit.

Temperatures of the Planets

It is likely that all the planets contain radioactive materials. When these materials break down, heat is generated. However, the amount of heat produced by this breakdown is very small. Most of the heat of a planet comes from the sun.

Since this is so, we should expect that the planets nearest the sun would be the hottest. The planets farthest from the sun we should expect to be the coldest. But this is not always true. Mercury, for example—the planet nearest the sun—is the hottest, just as we should expect it to be. But it is also a very cold planet. Mercury has very little, if any, atmosphere; therefore it cannot retain heat. The part turned away from the sun loses heat rapidly.

You may wonder how astronomers are able to measure the temperature of a planet that is millions of miles from us. They were unable to do this until the 1930's. In their laboratories men working with electricity found that an electric current could be made to flow in a circuit made of wires of two different materials —iron and copper, for example.

They twisted both ends of an iron and a copper wire together to form a loop. They broke the copper wire and fastened each end to a meter. One of the twists was put in ice water. When the other twist was heated, the meter showed that electricity was flowing in the circuit.

Many, many people improved on this first crude instrument, until they developed a temperature-measuring device, called a thermocouple, so sensitive that it can detect the heat from a candle 100 miles away. Such a device is attached to a telescope.

The telescope is aimed at a planet, and the light of the planet falls upon the thermocouple junction (twist). Changes in light intensity cause changes in the amount of electricity that is produced. These changes are related directly to temperature: the more energy in the form of light, the more heat—and the more electricity.

Another technique of measuring temperature uses radio astronomy. The warm surface of a planet produces radio waves. Through careful analysis of the waves, astronomers obtain a reliable indication of the temperature of the planet.

The temperatures of the various planets are given in the table. (Temperature readings will vary with the astronomer who takes them, the time that the investigation is made, and the type of instrument used.)

Planet	Temperature (Degrees F.)	Where Measured
MERCURY	700	Sunlit side
	−400 (?)	Dark side
VENUS	800	Surface
EARTH	57	Planetary temperature if measured from moon, for example
	−67	Stratosphere
MARS	−90 to +80	Hottest location
JUPITER	−225 (?)	⎫
SATURN	−250 (?)	⎪
URANUS	−290 (?)	⎬ Atmosphere
NEPTUNE	−325 (?)	⎪
PLUTO	−375 (?)	⎭

Temperatures on Mars change rapidly. At times certain areas have temperatures of about 80 degrees. When the sun goes down,

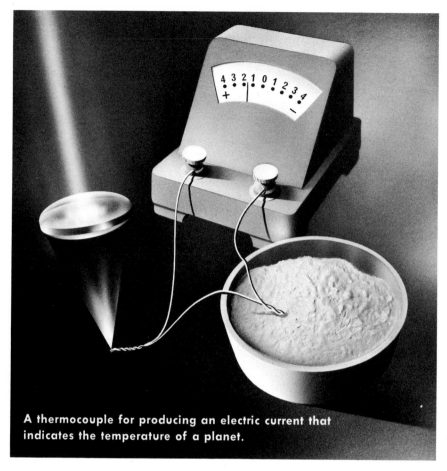

A thermocouple for producing an electric current that indicates the temperature of a planet.

the temperature in the same region drops probably a hundred degrees or more. This happens because there is not enough atmosphere to prevent heat loss.

The temperatures for the outer planets are the measurements of the atmospheres. We cannot be at all certain about the surface temperatures. Some people have suggested that the surface of any of these planets is very warm. They argue that the atmosphere is so thick that heat produced by the planet cannot escape. This heat, therefore, must have added up through the years. Other scientists argue that the surface is very cold—maybe as cold as anything can possibly be. They say that heat from the sun has never been able to reach the surface and that the planet itself does not produce much heat. We shall have to wait until more accurate measurements can be made before we know which idea is correct.

Apparently on Venus, with a temperature of 800 degrees F., heat has been stored up and does not escape readily. We may find the same process on the major planets. However, because of the greater distances from the sun, we should expect the maximum temperatures to be lower than that of Venus.

How Did the Planets Originate?

No one knows. But even though men have not found the answer to this question, they have made many attempts to answer it.

For example, some men say that the planets were pulled out of the sun. According to this explanation, a star came near our sun; its gravitational attraction pulled great globs of gas away from the sun; these masses of gas cooled and became the planets.

Other men have suggested that great explosions erupted on the sun. The explosions threw tremendous amounts of gas into space. The gases became the planets.

Another explanation is that space is full of tiny bits of matter. Long ago some of the matter started to gather together, and the process continued for billions of years. Gradually the collection of matter grew larger and larger. Finally the mass was so tremendous that a planet was formed.

As you learn more about astronomy, you will read more about these theories and about other theories that have been suggested. For centuries men have wondered where the earth came from—and where the other planets came from as well. Every attempt to find out has met with failure. But someday we shall know. Now that we are able to get out into space itself, we may find never-before-suspected clues that may bring us closer to the answer.

Speed in Orbit

Perhaps you have wondered why planets are able to keep in their orbits—why they don't wander off through space. Gravity and falling are both involved in the explanation. Suppose there were no gravity. If you threw a ball, the ball would go on and on, never returning to the earth. But there is gravity. You know this because if you drop a ball, it goes straight to the earth.

If you throw the ball instead of dropping it—if you give it some force of motion—the ball still falls to earth again. But this time it travels some distance before it falls to earth, because two forces are exerted upon it: gravity and its own motion. Throw the ball harder (give it more force). Now it goes farther before it hits the earth. If you could throw the ball hard enough (give it enough force), it would go over the horizon. It would continue around the earth and return from behind you. The ball would be "in free fall": it would be in orbit.

To help you understand this better, imagine that a gun were mounted a thousand miles or so above the sun, and that it were aimed tangent to the sun's surface. If a slow-moving bullet were shot from the gun, the bullet would fall into the sun. If the bullet were moving faster, it would cover more distance before it fell. If it were moving very, very rapidly, the bullet would still fall. But now it would move so that the curve of fall would carry it around the sun continuously, as shown in the diagram on the next page.

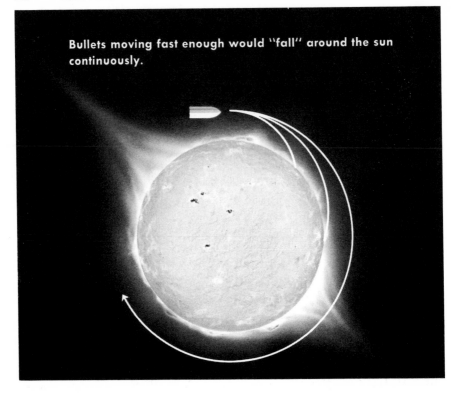

Bullets moving fast enough would "fall" around the sun continuously.

You might think of Mercury as a bullet moving about the sun. To move around and around without falling into the sun, it must move very fast. This is because Mercury is close to the sun and the gravitational attraction exerted upon Mercury is very great. Pluto, which is far from the sun, need not move so rapidly. The gravitational attraction upon it is much less than that upon Mercury. Planets stay in orbit (continue moving) because they move through space, where there are very few particles colliding with them to cause them to slow down.

The speeds of the planets in their paths about the sun are shown in the table. You will see that the farther a planet is from the sun, the slower the planet moves.

Planet	Mean Speed (Miles per Second)
MERCURY	29.8
VENUS	21.8
EARTH	18.5
MARS	15.0
JUPITER	8.1
SATURN	6.0
URANUS	4.2
NEPTUNE	3.4
PLUTO	2.9

Volume of the Planets

The planets vary a great deal in size. The earth is the planet we know best, so we compare the other planets with the earth. In the following table the volume of the earth is taken as 1. The volume of Jupiter is then 1300. This means that 1300 earths could be contained inside Jupiter, if Jupiter were a hollow ball. Pluto has a question mark beside it. This planet is so far away that we have been unable to obtain accurate measurements of its diameter. Therefore, we cannot be sure about its volume.

Planet	Volume (Earth = 1)
MERCURY	0.055
VENUS	0.888
EARTH	1.000
MARS	0.143
JUPITER	1321.946
SATURN	736.339
URANUS	51.716
NEPTUNE	38.776
PLUTO	0.094 (?)

93,000,000 miles to the sun

25,800,000,000,000 miles to Proxima Centauri, the star nearest the solar system

Other Solar Systems

The only planets that we have ever seen are those in our own solar system. But there are probably other planets in the universe. We know there are many stars that resemble our sun—that contain the same materials and are the same size, same temperature, and (probably) the same age. Astronomers believe that such stars have planets moving around them. If this is so, our part of the universe—the Milky Way Galaxy—contains thousands upon thousands of planets.

If there are other planets, we could never see them with earth-based instruments. We can see deep into space with our most powerful telescopes, but planets in orbit around other stars would be too small and too far away for us to see. The nearest possible planets are 26 million million miles from us. This is the distance to the nearest star beyond the solar system. We can see stars at this great distance, because they are very large and they produce their own light. Planets would be very dim because they produce no light of their own. We would be able to see them only by reflected starlight.

Astronomers have observed deflections in the motions of some stars that are believed to be caused by the attraction of nearby planets. But we have never seen such planets, nor do astronomers expect to see them. Telescopes of greater power than those we already have would be self-defeating because they would greatly magnify distortions. Space-based telescopes might help, but such possibilities are more nearly dreams than realities. We may never see these planets except by making space journeys that last for generations, missions that send ships beyond our solar system and out among the stars. Until that happens, we shall have to be content to believe there are other planets moving around other stars, even though we cannot prove their presence.

The solar system is in the Milky Way Galaxy.

MERCURY

diameter   3,100 miles

distance from the sun   36,000,000 miles

MERCURY IS THE FASTEST, THE SMALLEST, AND THE HOTTEST OF ALL THE PLANETS. In fact it is smaller than some of the satellites (moons) of the larger planets. Mercury is the planet closest to the sun.

Because it is so near the sun, the attraction of the sun is great. The planet moves very rapidly—so rapidly that the ancients named it for Mercury, the messenger of the gods. If Mercury did not move rapidly, it would be pulled into the sun. When it is nearest the sun (remember its orbit is elliptical and so its distance from the sun varies), Mercury moves 30 miles a second. This speed carries Mercury around the sun in 88 days, quite a bit less than the 365 days that the earth requires to make a circuit.

Rotation and Revolution

As all planets do, Mercury spins around on its axis. We used to think the planet completed one rotation in 88 days. We thought it had a rotation period (spinning on its axis) equal to its revolution period (moving around the sun)—and that consequently the same half of Mercury always faced the sun, the other half never receiving any sunlight.

However, investigations made with a large radio telescope located at Arecibo, Puerto Rico, and operated by Cornell University, indicate that Mercury rotates once in 59 days—considerably faster than was previously believed. A day on Mercury is 59 earth days long. The period of revolution of the planet around the sun is 88 days; the year on Mercury is 88 earth days long. This means that in the course of two years on Mercury, the planet experiences three days.

Only Mercury and Venus have long rotation periods. The other planets complete a rotation in a period ranging from 9 hours and 50 minutes for Jupiter to 6 days and 9 hours for Pluto.

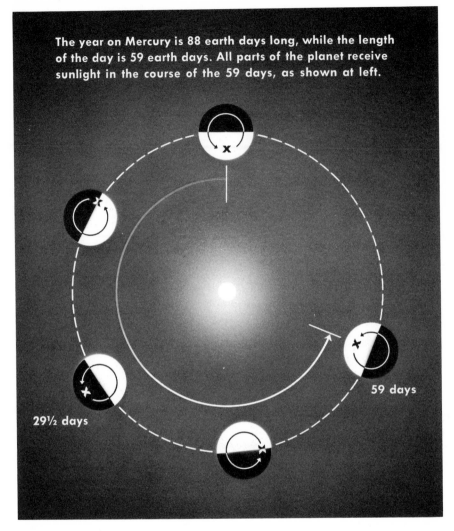

The year on Mercury is 88 earth days long, while the length of the day is 59 earth days. All parts of the planet receive sunlight in the course of the 59 days, as shown at left.

59 days

29½ days

Astronomers do not know why Mercury rotates so slowly. Some of them believe that the pull of the sun once caused great tides on Mercury. These were bulges of the solid material of the planet. The braking action of such tidal forces over hundreds of thousands of years has slowed down the planet's rotation.

Hot and Cold

The part of Mercury facing the sun has a long time to collect heat. It must get very hot indeed. Some measurements have told us that the hot part of Mercury has a temperature of 700 degrees. This is hot enough to set paper and wood on fire; hot enough to melt lead and tin. It is probably the highest temperature on any of the planets, except Venus.

But later on, the same part of Mercury will be away from the sun. It must be very cold, for it loses heat very fast. Some astronomers think that radioactivity in the crust of the planet may supply some heat. But this would not be enough to raise the temperature very much. The temperature on the dark side of Mercury may reach 400 degrees below zero. There is probably no other place in the entire solar system so cold as this. Pluto is very cold, we expect, because it is the planet farthest from the sun. However, many astronomers think it is warmer than the frigid side of Mercury, because Pluto may have an atmosphere that serves as a blanket to hold heat.

Evening and Morning Star

Usually when Mercury is well above the horizon, the sun is also in the sky; and the sun makes the heavens so bright that Mercury is not visible. But sometimes we can see Mercury with the unaided eye in the evening and in the early morning. When we do see Mercury, it is at elongation. Elongation is the position in its orbit when a planet is farthest east or west of the sun. When Mercury is at eastern elongation, we see it in the evening just after sunset. We then call it an evening star. This is because in days long past, people thought they were looking at a star. They did not know that planets existed; they called the objects that changed position in the sky the wandering stars.

When Mercury is at its western elongation, we see it in the

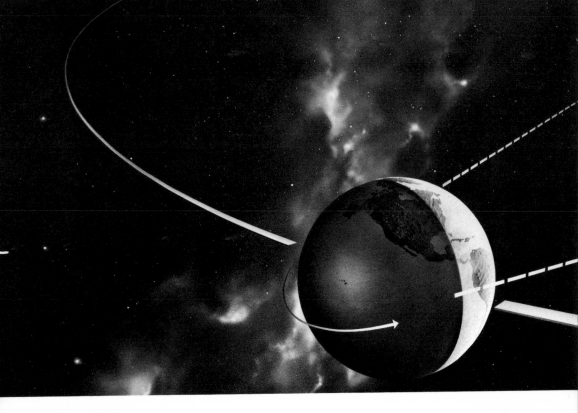

morning just before the sun rises. Then we call it a morning star.

An almanac will tell you when Mercury appears as a morning or evening star, and also the positions of the other planets.

Transit of the Sun

Sometimes Mercury passes between the earth and the sun, moving across the sun's disk. When this passage is observed, we say that the planet transits the sun. These passages can occur only around May 8 and November 10. In a period of 100 years there are about 13 transits of the sun by Mercury.

When Mercury transits the sun, it appears as a small black dot against the disk; however, a telescope is needed to see it. Do not attempt to look directly at the sun. In fact you must *never* look at the sun unless your eyes are protected with a piece of heavily smoked glass or some other high-density filter.

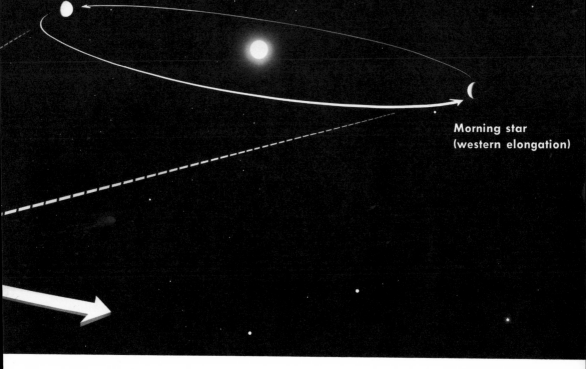

Morning star
(western elongation)

Phases

If we look at Mercury through a telescope, it appears to change shape. This is because we see different amounts of the lighted part of the planet. We say that it has phases. The illustration shows Mercury as we watch it travel about the sun. The different phases of Mercury cannot be observed without a telescope.

Surface

Because Mercury is so close to the sun, it is hard to observe the planet. In fact it is hard to study any of the planets. An astronomer may spend days, weeks, or months trying to see the details of a planet. And when he does get a clear view, the interval may be only a moment—little more than a fleeting glance. Opportunities for a clear view are rare because the light from the planet must pass through our atmosphere. The atmosphere contains many layers of air at different temperatures which disturb light passing through them. The atmosphere is rarely quiet. Images seen through it are wiggly, just as images seen through the air rising above a hot radiator are wiggly.

Astronomers make sketches to capture the features of the planet that they observe during their brief glimpses. The sketches vary a great deal from one astronomer to another. One may have seen the planet at a different time; or he may have imagined he saw formations not really there; or he may be quite unable to draw accurately those features that he saw.

Some astronomers have never seen Mercury well enough to draw features of it; while others have been able to make maps of it. One of these maps was made by Schiaparelli, an Italian astronomer. This map is very sketchy indeed. It merely suggests what the surface features might be like.

Later another map, more complete than Schiaparelli's, was drawn by Antoniadi, a French astronomer. At first glance this map appears to disagree strongly with the map drawn by Schiaparelli. After looking at both of them carefully, one can see that

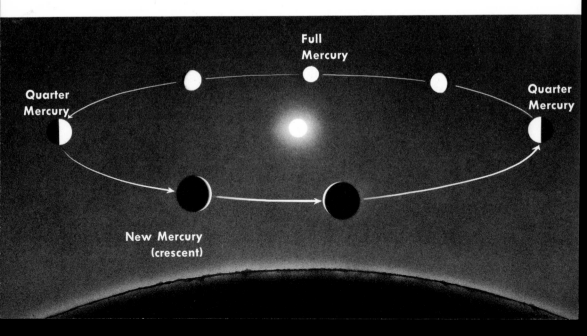

they agree much more than they differ. Not only is Antoniadi's map more complete, it is also better drawn.

Today we must still rely on sketches that astronomers draw. It is true that cameras and films have been developed which enable us to photograph many of the planets. Usually such photographs give us a more accurate idea of the make-up of a planet than do sketches; however, photographs of Mercury reveal none of its structure.

Atmosphere

Most astronomers believe that Mercury does not have an atmosphere. There are many reasons for this belief. (1) In order for a planet to have an atmosphere, it must have enough gravitational attraction to keep the atmosphere from escaping into space. Mercury has very little gravitational attraction—probably not enough to hold an atmosphere. (2) When particles in a gas are heated, they move more rapidly than when the gas is cool. The higher the temperature, the faster the particles move. Mercury is heated to such high temperatures that the particles of its atmosphere would move fast enough to escape from the planet. (3) We know that planets with atmospheres and clouds, such as Venus, reflect a large amount of sunlight. We also know that the moon, which has no atmosphere, reflects very little sunlight. The percentage of sunlight reflected by Mercury is about the same as that reflected by the moon; since the moon has no atmosphere, Mercury probably has none either.

Mercury would be a very uncomfortable planet to live on. The temperature might be pleasant along the line that separates night and day (the terminator). But one would have to get used to great extremes of temperature, to low gravitational attraction, and to the absence of an atmosphere, none of which would be possible for earthbound men.

VENUS

diameter 7,700 miles

distance from the sun 67,200,000 miles

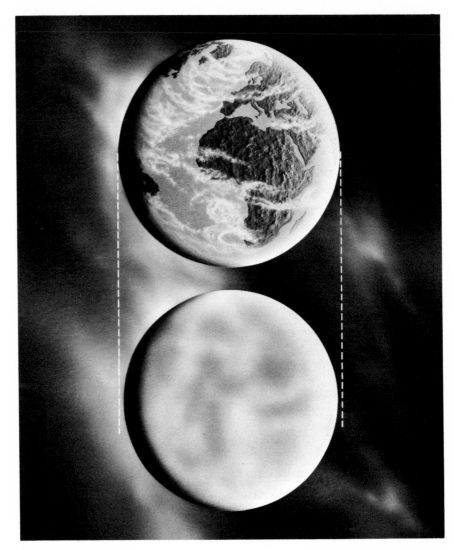

THE SUN IS THE BRIGHTEST OBJECT IN OUR SKY. Next in brightness is the moon; and next to the moon, at certain times, is Venus. Frequently we can see Venus during the day, and at night it sometimes is bright enough to cause shadows on the earth. People of ancient times knew this bright planet. It was so beautiful that they named it Venus after the Roman goddess of love and beauty.

Venus is about the same size as the earth. At its closest approach Venus is only about 25,700,000 miles away; it is the planet that gets closest to us. Venus moves about 22 miles a second. This is fast enough to carry it once around the sun in 225 days. In the time it takes the earth to go around the sun twice, Venus goes around the sun a little more than three times.

Phases

Venus moves around the sun in an orbit that is between the sun and the earth. For this reason we see varying amounts of the lighted half of Venus; and so for us this planet, when viewed through the telescope, goes through a complete cycle of phases. When it is close to the earth, we see Venus as a thin crescent. Because it is so near to us, the crescent is large and brilliant. As Venus moves away from us, the amount of the planet that we see increases; we see more and more of it. But because it is farther from us, it appears smaller and is much less brilliant. We see Venus best when it is close to us, even though we see less of the planet at that time.

Because Venus is between the earth and the sun, we cannot see it at midnight, just as we cannot see the sun. The best times for viewing Venus are just after sunset and just before sunrise. Because this is so, we often call Venus an evening star or a morning star, just as we do Mercury. In ancient days many observers did not know that Venus is a planet. They believed that Venus, when seen at evening, was one star, and when seen at morning was an

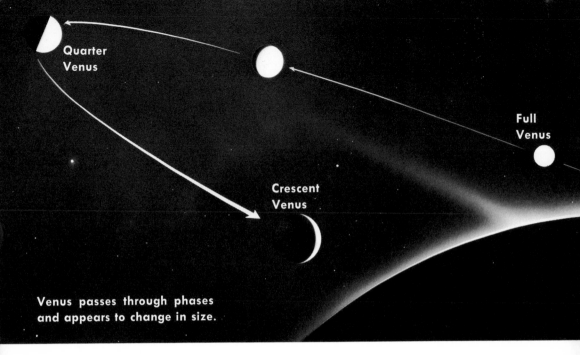

Venus passes through phases and appears to change in size.

entirely different star. They called the evening "star" Hesperus and the morning "star" Phosphorus.

There are 72 days between the brightest appearance of Venus in the evening and its brightest appearance in the morning. For Venus to move beyond the sun and return once again to its place of brightest illumination in the skies of evening, 512 days are needed. The time is greater than 225 days because at the same time that Venus is going around the sun, the earth is also revolving; and it takes this length of time for both to return to the same position relative to the sun and to each other.

Atmosphere

We have never seen the surface of Venus, for it is obscured by an opaque atmosphere. The atmosphere appears laden with clouds that show no difference in color to the unaided eye. These may be so opaque that bright sunlight cannot penetrate to the solid surface. The skies of Venus probably are heavily overcast every day of the year.

One of the best proofs of the presence of an atmosphere on Venus is obtained by observing the planet when it is almost in line between the earth and the sun. When the planet is in this position we see a twilight arc all around it; the horns of the crescent are greatly extended. We believe that this effect could be produced only by the deflection of sunlight by an atmosphere.

But what makes up this atmosphere? The earth's atmosphere is made up of nitrogen and oxygen for the most part. We cannot be sure about the materials that are in the atmosphere of Venus. It is quite impossible for us to probe through the atmosphere to the surface of this planet. Studies of that part of the atmosphere above the dense Venusian clouds reveal a very high percentage of carbon dioxide. There appears to be more of this gas below the dense cloud layer, and there are also traces of water vapor.

Astronomers know that the atmosphere of Venus contains carbon dioxide because of clues that spectroscopes on earth and in space probes reveal. A spectroscope is an instrument that analyzes light by the colors of which it is made. For example, an astronomer can tell whether a gas is oxygen, nitrogen, carbon dioxide, or some other material by the kind of light it produces. All clues so far indicate that the main gas in the atmosphere of Venus is carbon dioxide.

Traces of water vapor on Venus were detected by instruments carried by balloons high into the upper atmosphere of the earth. Oxygen and nitrogen have never been identified on Venus. However, these gases may exist there, and we may discover them when our tools improve. For the present, carbon dioxide is the only material definitely known to exist in quantity on Venus. This is interesting, for the amount of carbon dioxide in our own atmosphere is very small—only about 3/100 of 1 per cent (0.03%).

Scientists would like to know why there is so much of this gas in the atmosphere of Venus. They also would like to know whether the part of the atmosphere close to the planetary surface is the same as the top of the atmosphere.

Rotation Period

When you look at Venus, the entire planet appears the same color at all times, with no variations. This makes it very difficult to tell how long it takes the planet to turn around. When we look at Mars, on the contrary, we can pick out a detail on the surface; we can time the interval that passes before that detail appears again, and so we know the rotation period of Mars. But what can an astronomer do when there are no details to be seen?

F. E. Ross of the Mount Wilson Observatory in California took photos of Venus through a filter that allowed only ultraviolet light to strike the film. (Ultraviolet is the kind of light energy that gives you a sunburn.) When he looked at the developed film, he could see differences in the light: some places were dark, others were bright. But the regions were so numerous and they changed so rapidly that Ross was unable to tell how long it took Venus to rotate.

In 1964 astronomers at the Arecibo radio astronomy station in Puerto Rico investigated the rotation period of Venus. They found it to be about 244 days, which is longer than the time it takes the planet to go around the sun. Venus appears to be rotating in a direction opposite to the direction in which the other planets rotate. We say that its rotation is "retrograde."

Temperature

Several years ago two astronomers at Mount Wilson—Pettit and Nicholson—made careful studies of the temperatures on Venus, or rather of the temperatures of the upper clouds. They found that the temperature of the sunlit side was about 130 degrees. The night side was not terribly cold—about 13 degrees below zero. Since the difference between the two temperatures was not very great, the astronomers could infer that the planet was rotating and that all parts of it were alternately heated and cooled. If the periods of rotation and revolution were equal, one side would be very, very hot, the other unbearably cold—much hotter than 130 degrees and much colder than 13 degrees below zero.

Pettit and Nicholson obtained their information about temperatures by studying the light of stars or the sunlight reflected by planets. Today temperatures are measured by analyzing radio waves that are received from planets and natural satellites. Movement of gases in the atmosphere of a planet, if there is any, and of the atoms of the surface, produce the radio waves that provide the information.

Radio waves have been picked up from Venus. They indicate that the temperature of the planet is considerably higher than we previously thought. It is probable that there is a wide range of temperatures; however, there is much uncertainty about this conclusion. One reason for this is that many astronomers are not positive whether we are measuring the temperature of the surface or the temperature of the lower layers of the atmosphere.

Mariner space probes that came within a few thousand miles of Venus, and Russian capsules that landed on the surface, gave more data. Instruments aboard them measured the temperature of the planet, and the information was sent to the earth by radio. The surface temperature of Venus revealed by these probes, and by other techniques, was found to be close to 800 degrees F. This is the over-all temperature. There may be limited areas where the temperature is considerably lower, as indicated by radio astronomy techniques.

The high temperatures may result because the atmosphere of the planet permits short-wave radiant energy from the sun to pass through to the surface. There the energy becomes long-wave heat. This is held in by the atmosphere, and so the temperature builds up.

Transit of the Sun

Occasionally the earth and Venus are on the same side of the sun. When we look at Venus at such times, the planet is usually north or south of the sun. But infrequently Venus passes directly in front of the sun and we see the planet as a black speck moving across the solar disk, just as we sometimes see Mercury. When this occurs, we say that Venus transits the sun. The first predicted and observed transit by Venus occurred in 1639. There have been four transits since then; the next one will take place on June 8, 2004. Astronomers look forward to these events, for they can check some of their facts by observing the transit carefully.

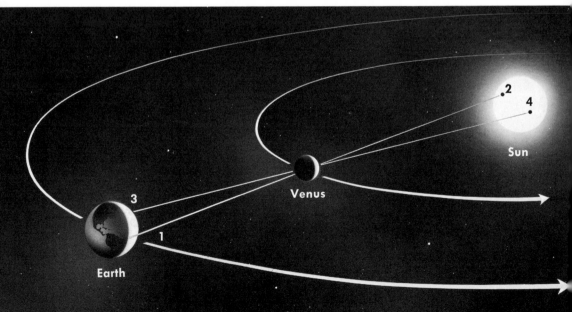

Venus transits the sun

For example, a precise indication of the distance from the earth to the sun can be obtained by using the black spot which is Venus as a reference point on the sun. The diagram shows Venus transiting the sun. An observer at position 1 would see Venus at 2 against the background of the sun. An observer at position 3 would see the planet at 4. By knowing the distance between 1 and 3, the two points on the earth, scientists can compute the distance to the sun.

The Ashen Light

Frequently when we see a crescent moon, the rest of the moon is softly lighted. We say that "the old moon is in the new moon's arms." A long time ago scientists learned the reason for the soft light from the moon. When in the crescent phase the moon is almost in a line between the earth and the sun. The sun shines brightly on the earth. Some of this sunlight reflects back to the moon, lighting the part turned away from the sun.

Venus sometimes appears in a soft, grayish light. Some astronomers have suggested that this "ashen light" of Venus might be explained in the way that the soft light of the moon is explained: they say the light may be reflected from the earth. But many authorities disagree with this explanation. They say the planet is too far away for light reflected from the earth to reach it—and so the light must be caused by something we do not understand.

Another possible explanation is that the ashen light is very much like our aurora displays, known as the northern and southern lights. We believe that these polar lights of the earth are caused by electrified particles that stream out from the sun. The particles strike the upper atmosphere of the earth, causing it to glow. Since Venus is closer to the sun than is the earth, the flow of particles from the sun would be more intense. We know Venus has an atmosphere. Therefore many people believe that the ashen light could be some kind of aurora glow. In order for us to see it, however, the glow would have to be much more intense and much more extensive than the northern lights we see on our own planet. Information from the Mariner vehicles does not give much support to such a theory.

Venus is indeed a planet of many mysteries. The ashen light is only one of the unanswered questions that astronomers are trying to solve. They would like to know the precise composition of the atmosphere at all altitudes; the temperatures at all levels; the nature of the crust and internal structure. Maybe when we learn how to use radio astronomy and space probes more effectively, these tools will reveal knowledge that will help us answer such questions.

EARTH

diameter   7,918 miles

distance from the sun   92,900,000 miles

THE EARTH IS A MIDDLE-SIZED PLANET. Mercury, Venus, Mars, and Pluto are smaller than the earth. Jupiter, Saturn, Uranus, and Neptune are larger. But even though it is not the biggest planet, the earth is the most important one to us. So far as we know, the earth is the only planet upon which life exists. The name probably comes from *eorthe*, an Anglo-Saxon word.

The earth is the third planet out from the sun. Mercury and Venus are closer to the sun than we are; the rest of the planets are farther from the sun. The earth is the first planet, counting outward from the sun, that has a satellite (the moon) revolving about it. As we continue farther out, we shall find that all the other planets have satellites except Pluto.

When we observe Mercury and Venus, we see the planets either in the evening or early in the morning just before sunrise. We never see these planets at midnight because we are turned away from the sun and also from the planets at that time, as shown in the diagram.

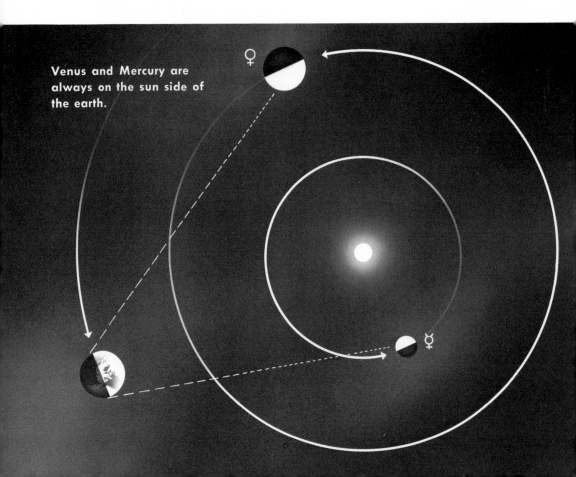

Venus and Mercury are always on the sun side of the earth.

We can see Mars, Jupiter, and Saturn all through the night. We cannot see them every night—only when they are in the right positions.

The earth's diameter is given as 7918 miles. This is the mean diameter. The earth is not spherical like a ball; it is somewhat flattened and bulged. The diameter from pole to pole is 7899 miles. The diameter from one side of the equator to the other is 7926 miles. Instead of calling the earth a sphere, astronomers call it an oblate spheroid.

The earth is the planet about which we have the most information. For example, we know that it is made of three primary substances: water, land, and air—or the hydrosphere, geosphere, and atmosphere.

Surface

Some 75 per cent of the surface of the earth is covered with water. It is entirely likely that our planet contains more water than any other planet in the solar system; and it may be the only planet that contains this vital substance in any effective amount. The only other places in the solar system where water has been found are on Mars and Venus. Venus seems to have only traces —and the total amount of water on Mars is not much. It is probably no more than enough to fill the basin of Lake Erie. (At other locations in the solar system there may be water that we have been unable to identify.)

The solid portion of the earth is the geosphere. Men have never probed deep into the earth, and so our knowledge of its interior is limited. It is believed that the center of the earth is composed of nickel and iron in a semimolten state. The only part of the solid portion that we have studied extensively is the outer mantle. A layer of loose rocks, sand, gravel, and soil covers much of the earth. Solid rock has been weathered for millions of years by wind and water, and has been broken down into smaller pieces and into small granules that make up the bulk of the soil. Beneath these weathered materials are layers of original rock—granite and basalt, which probably formed when the earth came into being.

Surrounding the earth is an envelope of gases that make up our atmosphere. No doubt the atmosphere has changed in composition during the hundreds of millions of years that the earth has existed. However, at the present time the atmosphere contains two main gases—nitrogen and oxygen (nitrogen, 78 per cent; oxygen, 21 per cent). Of the remaining 1 per cent, 0.03 per cent is carbon dioxide and 0.97 per cent is made up of helium, argon, krypton, xenon—the rare gases, as they are often called.

Motions

The earth is our clock; but it is not a very good one. If a year (365 days) were the exact time required for the earth to travel around the sun, all would be well. The year would come out to an exact number of days. Actually the earth takes about one quarter of a day more than a year to complete the journey. But this extra ¼ day is not in our calendar; it was just dropped. If we were to continue in this manner, dropping a quarter of a day each year, after a number of years the earth would not be in position in March (let us say) for the beginning of spring. Spring would be starting during the winter months, and our calendar would be out of step with the seasons. So we adjust our calendar by adding a day during leap year.

The earth takes 365 days, 5 hours, 48 minutes, and 46 seconds to go around the sun. The journey is a long one—about 600 million miles. To complete the journey in this time, the earth moves at a mean speed of 18.5 miles a second.

To get some idea of the way the earth moves around the sun,

we can use a ball and a table top. We shall say that the sun is at the center of the table. Move the ball in a large circle around the central sun. The table top is the plane of the earth's orbit around the sun.

Of course there is no table top in outer space. But there is an imaginary curve traced out by the earth. The region enclosed inside the curve is the plane of the earth's orbit.

While the earth is revolving around the sun, it is spinning like a top. There is an imaginary axle, or axis, passing from pole to pole, around which it turns. This axis is not vertical to the plane of the earth's orbit—that is, straight up and down. If it were, there would be no change of seasons; we should have the same season year in and year out. The axis is tilted 23½ degrees from that vertical line. Astronomers say that the axis of the earth is tilted 23½ degrees from a line vertical to the plane of the earth's orbit. The north end of the axis points toward the North Star during the entire year.

Because the axis is tilted in this manner, we have a regular change of seasons. During summer the part of the earth north of the equator—the northern hemisphere—is tilted toward the sun.

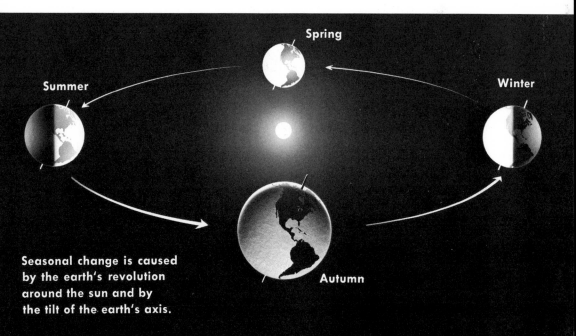

Seasonal change is caused by the earth's revolution around the sun and by the tilt of the earth's axis.

During winter the same part of the earth is tilted away from the sun. During spring and fall the tilt of the axis is neither toward nor away from the sun.

Interestingly enough we are closest to the sun during winter in the northern hemisphere. We are about 3 million miles closer at that time than we are during summer. Nearness to or farness from the sun is not the reason for the seasons. The main cause is the tilt of the earth's axis. If we are tilted toward the sun, the sunlight is concentrated in a limited area; if we are tilted away from the sun, the sunlight is spread out. The part of the earth that is tilted toward the sun has summer, no matter whether the sun is closest to us at that time or farthest away.

A simple experiment with a flashlight will help you understand. Hold a flashlight at a right angle to the wall and a little distance from it, so that the spot of light is small. Then tilt the flashlight, causing the light to spread out. The first case represents summer: the light is concentrated. The second case represents winter: the light is spread out.

The earth rotates around its axis, spinning like a top. One rotation is completed in a single day. The time required for an exact rotation is actually a little less than a day; it is 23 hours, 56 minutes and 4 seconds. But during one rotation the earth has moved enough in its orbit so that 4 minutes more are required for the sun to be in the same position it was 24 hours earlier. Rotation produces day and night. One half of the earth is always lighted by the sun. The half of the earth toward the sun is in daylight; the other half is in darkness.

The earth rotates from west to east. If you were above the North Pole looking down upon the earth, the motion would be opposite to the direction in which the hands of a clock move; it would be counterclockwise.

Sunrise occurs not because the sun actually rises. It occurs

because the rotation of the earth carries you into the sunlight.
Therefore when you first see the sun, it is on your horizon. Later
in the day it is overhead. In the evening the turning of the earth
carries you away from the sun and into night. The last position
in which you glimpse the sun is on the opposite horizon. The
earth turns a little more, and your view of the sun has been cut
off: night has arrived. Day and night, sunrise and sunset, the high
location of the sun at noon—all these are caused by the rotation
of the earth.

While the earth revolves and rotates, it moves in other ways.
The tendency of the spinning earth is to remain in a fixed position; but the moon, which is very close to us, pulls upon the earth.

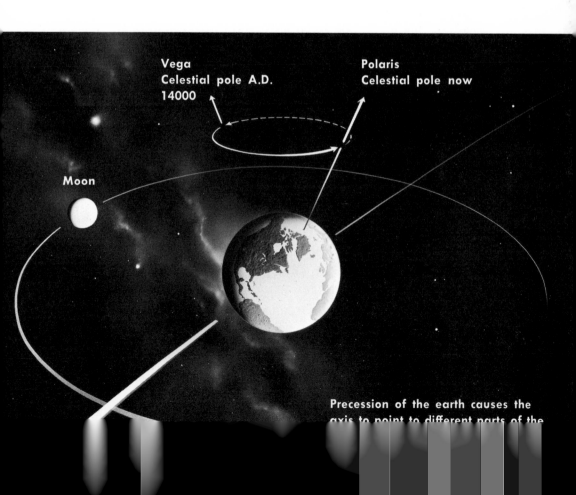

Vega
Celestial pole A.D.
14000

Polaris
Celestial pole now

Moon

Precession of the earth causes the
axis to point to different parts of the

The effect of this pull is to tip the planet over. However, the spinning of the earth prevents it from tipping over. Nevertheless the pull of the moon does cause the axis of the earth to outline a cone in space, as shown in the diagram. Right now the axis of the earth points almost toward Polaris, the North Star. But 12,000 years from now the axis will point more nearly toward Vega, the bright star in the constellation Lyra. It takes 26,000 years for the axis to go all the way around and to return to the point where it started—back in the direction of Polaris, the present North Star.

This motion, which is called precession, is a nuisance for astronomers. It means that their measurements of the locations of stars must be corrected from time to time.

It is hard to believe that the earth is spinning around, moving rapidly through space, and precessing on its axis. As you sit reading this book, you have no feeling of motion at all. That is because you and everything around you are moving in the same fashion. If you were moving and everything else close by were still, you would sense motion. That is what happens when you are riding in a car or train. When you are in a high-flying airplane—which goes much faster than a car or train—you do not sense the motion because you are so far from objects that are standing still.

MARS

diameter   4,200 miles

distance from the sun   141,500,000 miles

TWO TINY SATELLITES REVOLVE ABOUT MARS. Their names are from mythology, as is the name of Mars itself. They are called Deimos (panic) and Phobos (fear)—the companions of Mars, the god of war.

Mars is the only planet on which we have seen land formations. All the other planets are either too far away for us to see any details or covered with opaque clouds.

In 1877 Schiaparelli, the Italian astronomer, announced that he had seen straight lines on Mars. He called them channels. The Italian word for channels is *canali*. Ever since then men have been looking for these channels of Mars. Some men believed Schiaparelli meant that he had seen canals. There is a great difference between a channel and a canal. A channel might be a natural waterway; for example, when a stream cuts through sand and gravel, it digs a channel. A canal is a waterway made by creatures having intelligence. No *canals* have ever been photographed. Many astronomers have seen formations that might be *channels* of some sort. But there is no proof that there are canals on Mars.

Another reason that Mars interests people is that life may exist there. The American astronomer Percival Lowell, who died in 1916, believed there was life on Mars. In fact he wrote several books that explained his beliefs. Many astronomers support Lowell's theories even today. Since his time Mars has been observed carefully, and Mariners have sent us photographs of the surface; but no evidence to prove that life of any kind exists there has been found.

There is a possibility that some kind of plant life lives on Mars. Sections of the planet are green part of the year, and then the same sections turn brown. The color change may be caused by plants that grow and then die. No other signs that might be caused by plant life have been observed.

Some people believe that animals of some kind exist on this neighbor of ours. Perhaps you have talked with such people or read reports they have written. Listen and read carefully. You will find that people who tell us there are animals on Mars do not use facts in their explanations. There are so far no facts at all to support a belief in animal life on the planet.

Surface

Mars is often called the red planet. If you have seen it without a telescope you know why, for it has a definite reddish color. Through a telescope the color is a mottled red.

The light that comes to us from Mars is reflected sunlight, as is the light from all the planets. Mars acts like a great screen that reflects to the earth some of the light falling upon it. Since the light is reddish, we know that parts of the surface of Mars must be red. Several explanations of the red color have been made.

Some astronomers think that Mars is covered with dustlike material composed mostly of iron oxide. (Iron rust, which you have seen frequently on exposed metal, is iron oxide.) These astronomers say that the metals that once existed on Mars have rusted away and iron oxide has accumulated.

Men have experimented in laboratories to see if they could produce the same kind of light that is received from Mars. They covered a surface with different kinds of crumbled rock and then allowed sunlight to fall on it. The reflected light was studied carefully and compared with the light from Mars. There were several different rocks which produced light a little like that from Mars. But the closest match was produced by felsite, a kind of rock that is found in many places on the earth. The experimenters concluded that there is a strong possibility that the red areas of Mars are covered by felsite.

In 1965 Mariner IV took the first close-up pictures of Mars. This is number 11, the best of the 21 sent back by the vehicle.

In the summer of 1965 Mariner IV, a planetary probe, successfully photographed and transmitted to the earth pictures of about 1 per cent of the Martian surface. The Mariner IV photographs, and other pictures sent back by Mariners VI and VII in 1969, reveal no canals nor signs of life. Indeed the surface of Mars appears to be very much like the surface of the moon: barren, covered with large and small craters—certainly not a pleasant environment at all.

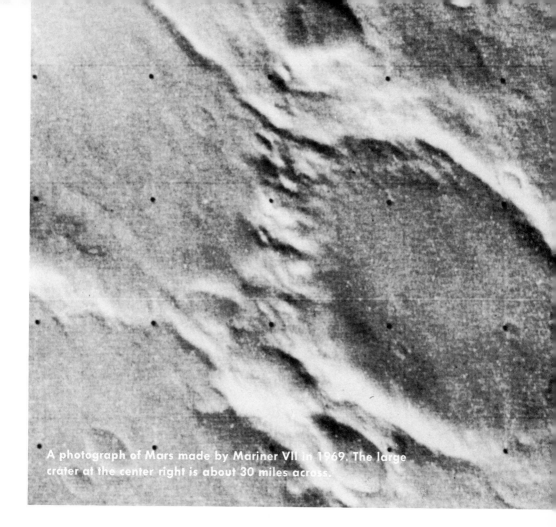

A photograph of Mars made by Mariner VII in 1969. The large crater at the center right is about 30 miles across.

Atmosphere

We are certain that Mars has an atmosphere. But the only material that we are positive exists in it is carbon dioxide. The atmosphere of Mars contains considerably more of this gas than our own atmosphere does. There is also considerable evidence that methane and ammonia are present.

Astronomers are not quite sure whether the atmosphere contains nitrogen. This gas has never been identified on Mars. But it is a heavy gas and so could not escape easily. The gravitational attraction of Mars is not strong enough to hold the lighter gases, such as hydrogen and helium; but it is strong enough to hold nitrogen.

Perhaps you know that the pressure of the atmosphere here on the earth is about 15 pounds on every square inch. On Mars the pressure is much less—so low that the water in our bodies would boil, making existence impossible. We would blow up like balloons, growing larger and larger, and finally we would burst. If and when men go to Mars, they will have to live inside space suits—either that or they must live inside containers in which higher pressure can be maintained.

Motions

The axis of Mars is tilted. The earth's axis is tilted 23½ degrees from a line vertical to the plane of its orbit. The axis of Mars is tilted a bit more—slightly over 25 degrees. Because of this tilt Mars has changes of seasons as it goes about the sun. It takes 687 days for Mars to go around the sun—almost twice as long as the earth requires. Seasons on Mars are therefore about twice as long as they are on the earth. A year on Mars is 687 earth days long. If you are twelve years old here on the earth, you would be only a little more than six years old if you were a Martian.

There are two reasons why the year on Mars is longer than a year on the earth. Mars is farther from the sun than we are, and so its path is longer. The path of the earth around the sun is about 600 million miles; the path of Mars is almost 900 million miles. Also Mars moves more slowly than we do. The earth moves 18.5 miles every second; Mars moves 15 miles a second.

While Mars revolves about the sun, this red planet also spins on its axis like a top. The rotation, or spinning, of the earth causes day and night. Since Mars spins, it has day and night also. The earth makes a rotation in 23 hours and 56 minutes; Mars makes a rotation in 24 hours, 37 minutes, and 22.6 seconds. The day on Mars is just a bit longer than it is on the earth. And just as the length of daylight at any given location on the earth changes through the year, so the length of daylight changes on Mars.

Distance

The distance of Mars from the earth varies. Sometimes it is very far from us—as much as 249 million miles. At other times Mars is only 35 million miles from us. Close approaches like this occur about every 15 years. When Mars is close to us, we say it is in opposition, because the sun is on one side of the earth and the red planet is on the opposite side. Astronomers look forward to "favorable" oppositions such as those represented in the diagram, because when Mars is closest to us its image is much larger.

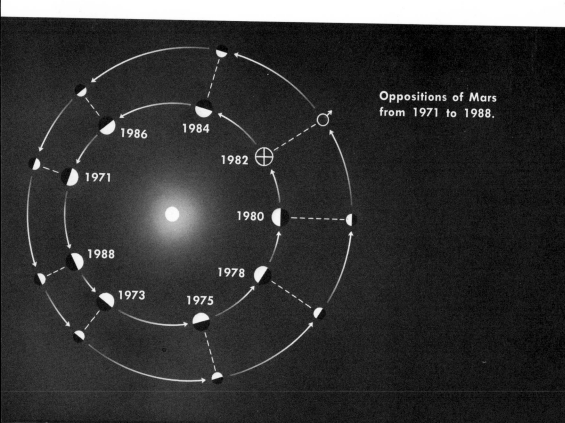

Oppositions of Mars from 1971 to 1988.

JUPITER

diameter   88,700 miles

distance from the sun   483,300,000 miles

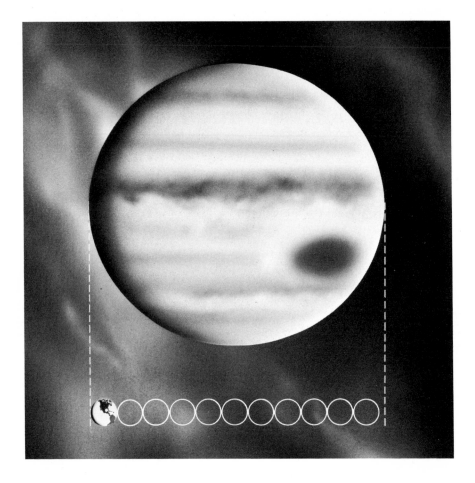

JUPITER IS THE LARGEST OF ALL THE PLANETS. It has 12 satellites moving around it—more than any other planet. The name, given by the ancients, stands for the king of the gods. If Jupiter were hollow, all the other planets could be melted and poured into it and there would be room left over. It is so large that 1300 earths could be contained in its volume, as we mentioned earlier.

The diameter given above is the mean dimension. When careful measurements are made, we find that Jupiter is flattened quite a bit. The diameter at the equator is about 5000 miles greater than the polar diameter. This great difference is pretty good evidence that Jupiter is made up largely of solidly frozen and semifrozen gases, with a small solid core. In fact we cannot be certain that Jupiter has a solid surface at all.

Atmosphere

Jupiter's atmosphere is not especially thick or extensive. Many astronomers believe the main components are probably hydrogen and helium, materials that we cannot readily identify. We can detect ammonia and methane, however.

Perhaps you have sniffed ammonia in household cleaning supplies and know how acrid it smells. Methane is a gas found in deep pits and around swampy, stagnant pools. It is explosive in the presence of oxygen and is also poisonous.

Ammonia is made up of hydrogen and nitrogen; methane is composed of hydrogen and carbon. Hydrogen is probably the most plentiful material on Jupiter. Indeed hydrogen is the most abundant material in the universe. The earth has lost most of the hydrogen that existed at one time in its atmosphere. Jupiter has not lost it; the hydrogen is still there, although most of it has combined with other materials.

Composition

We cannot be at all sure about the composition of Jupiter. We have observed the atmosphere and determined some of the gases in it. Also we have seen cloudlike formations in the atmosphere that we believe to be made of frozen ammonia gas. Beyond this we know very little about the structure of this huge planet.

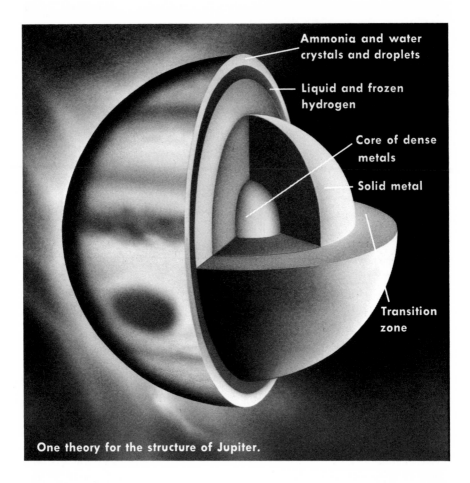

Ammonia and water crystals and droplets

Liquid and frozen hydrogen

Core of dense metals

Solid metal

Transition zone

One theory for the structure of Jupiter.

Some astronomers believe that the atmosphere of Jupiter is 200 or more miles deep. The atmosphere blends into ammonia crystals and semifrozen hydrogen. This layer could blend into a transition zone that may contain a mixture of stony and metallic materials. The central part of the planet is believed to be made of two metallic layers, the innermost one containing the more dense metals, the less dense ones surrounding it. If these ideas are true, Jupiter certainly is a barren, desolate world. Space travelers of the future will keep clear of this forbidding planet.

Motions

Jupiter is the largest of all the planets. Also Jupiter spins faster than any of them. The earth takes about 24 hours to make a single turn around its axis; Jupiter makes a rotation in only 9 hours, 50 minutes, and 30 seconds. Such a short rotation period means that the equatorial section is moving 28,000 miles per hour. The equatorial region of the earth moves about 1,000 miles an hour.

This means that any particular part of the surface of Jupiter would be in sunlight for only about 5 hours and in darkness for the same length of time.

You recall that the closer a planet is to the sun, the faster it moves about the sun. Mercury, the closest planet, goes around the sun in 88 days; Venus takes 225 days; Earth 365 days, or 1 year; Mars 687 days. Jupiter, the next planet out from the sun, takes 12 years to go around the sun only once. If you are eleven earth years old, you would still be waiting for your first birthday if you lived on Jupiter.

Surface Features

Jupiter appears as a very bright object in the sky. Of all the planets only Venus and sometimes Mars are brighter. Through the telescope Jupiter is very colorful. Parts of it are yellow, other sections brick-red. There is usually a broad yellow band along the equator. Bands farther from the equator change to red and brown.

Frequently spots of color are visible. One of the largest of these was first reported reliably about 75 years ago, although records indicate that men knew about it long before. It is a reddish area, about 30,000 miles long and 7,000 miles wide.

No one knows the cause of the red spot. Some believe it is the

cone of a great volcano piercing the atmosphere. But this explanation is not a good one, for the spot drifts about, changing
position from time to time. A volcano could not change position.

The red spot may be some sort of solid material floating in the
atmosphere. Or it may be a peculiar kind of cloud formation
that has persisted through the years.

Radio Noise

A few years ago Drs. Burke and Franklin of the Carnegie
Institution of Washington detected radio noises produced on
Jupiter.

The presence of radio noise does not mean that there are radio
broadcasting stations on this huge planet. It does indicate that
disturbances occur on Jupiter—perhaps in the atmosphere—that
cause radio energy to be created. These astronomers, and others,
are continuing this research. They will probe more deeply into
the mysteries of this planet, and other planets. Perhaps they will
be able to determine information about the temperatures, the
nature of the crusts, and other aspects of the planets that are
rather hazy at the present time.

The radio telescope is a new tool of research—one that we are
learning how to use more effectively. It has already revealed to
us aspects of the universe never before suspected.

SATURN

diameter   75,100 miles

distance from the sun   886,000,000 miles

SATURN IS THE MOST BEAUTIFUL OF ALL THE PLANETS. It is the outermost planet that we can see with the unaided eye. Before the invention of the telescope in the early part of the seventeenth century, people believed there were no planets beyond Saturn.

62

Saturn is covered with a dense atmosphere composed of methane and ammonia, hydrogen and helium. Because it is so far from the sun, Saturn's temperature is very low. It is so low that the ammonia of the atmosphere is in the form of ice crystals. Therefore methane is the gas most prominent in the atmosphere. Saturn is a very large planet; its diameter is more than 9 times greater than the earth's. But the solid core of the planet is quite small—only about 3 times the earth's diameter. Probably a great layer of frozen ammonia surrounds the solid core of the planet. And covering the ice there is probably a thick layer of atmosphere. It may be so extensive that it is half the total diameter.

Saturn is the most flattened of all the planets. You will recall that there is 27 miles difference between the polar and equatorial diameters of the earth. The equatorial diameter of Saturn is 75,000 miles; the polar diameter is 67,000 miles. There is a difference of 8,000 miles between the two. So a model of Saturn will have to be flatter than for any of the other planets.

People of ancient times noted that this remote planet moved very slowly against the starry background. They called the planet Saturn after the god of time. Saturn does move slowly, for it takes 29½ years to go around the sun once—a year on Saturn would be almost 11,000 earth days long. It would contain many more Saturn days than that, for the planet spins very fast on its axis. It makes a rotation in just over 10 hours—so a year on Saturn would contain some 25,000 Saturn days. You would need a thick calendar if you were living on Saturn!

Satellites and Rings

Ten satellites of Saturn have been discovered. Number 10, which is called Janus, was identified in 1966 by the French astronomer A. Dollfus. It appears to be about 300 miles in diameter and located some 100,000 miles from the planet itself.

Titan, the largest satellite, is some 2980 miles in diameter. You recall that the earth's satellite is 2160 miles across. As far as we know, Titan is the only satellite in the solar system that possesses an atmosphere; methane has been identified on several occasions.

The names of Saturn's satellites are fascinating. In order of their distance from the planet, they are Janus, Mimas, Enceladus,

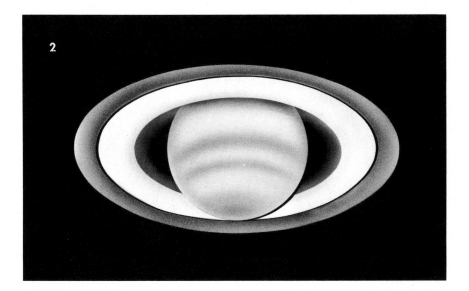

Tethys, Dione, Rhẹa, Titan, Hyperion, Iapetus, and Phoebe—
which is over 8 million miles away.

In addition to 10 satellites, Saturn has a beautiful system of
rings. At one time astronomers believed there was only one ring.
We know now that there are three of them. All the rings are
arranged on a plane extending from the equator, like a disk

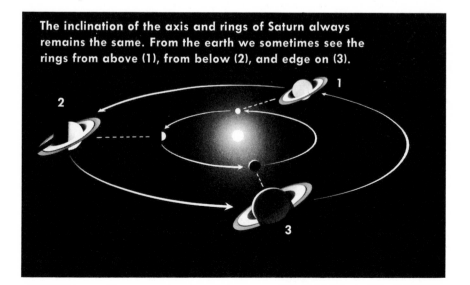

The inclination of the axis and rings of Saturn always
remains the same. From the earth we sometimes see the
rings from above (1), from below (2), and edge on (3).

around the planet. The distance from one side of the rings to the other is 170,000 miles. Some astronomers think that their essential thickness is about 10 miles—certainly not more than 40; while estimates made by other astronomers are as great as 100 miles. The outer, or A, ring is about 10,000 miles wide.

As we move toward the planet, we pass through a gap and then approach another ring. This is the B ring. It is about 16,000 miles wide and is the brightest of all the rings.

Between the B ring and the planet is the crepe ring. It was called the crepe ring because the materials in it are spread so thinly that the planet itself can be seen through the ring.

The rings are not solid. They are made of fine particles, perhaps the size of small grains of sand. Each particle moves in an orbit around the mother planet. The particles in the inner part of each ring move much faster than those near the outer edge.

We cannot be certain about the origin of Saturn's rings. We believe that they may have been a satellite at one time. An astronomer named Roche has figured that if a satellite comes within a certain distance of a planet, the satellite will shatter. The rings of Saturn are inside that limit. Perhaps a satellite of Saturn moved toward the planet, reached the Roche limit, and so shattered into millions of small particles.

Still another theory about these rings has been presented: that the particles making the rings never collected together to produce a moon. This is possible; however, the Roche explanation is more widely accepted.

We do not always see the rings of Saturn when we view the planet through a telescope. At times in the 29½-year period the rings are edge-on toward us; at such times we cannot see them. At other times we can see the rings very clearly, either above the planet or below it. The diagram shows why this is so.

URANUS

diameter   29,500 miles

distance from the sun   1,783,000,000 miles

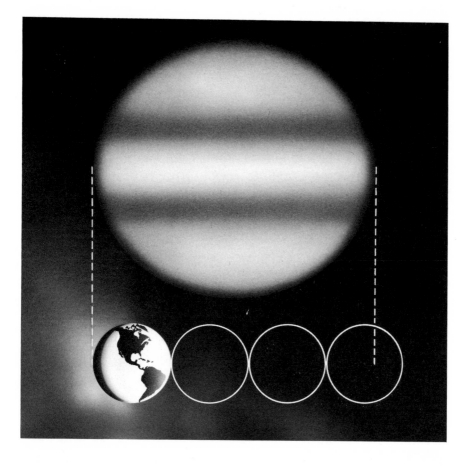

IN ANCIENT TIMES, SEVEN WAS A MAGIC NUMBER. Therefore there was every reason why there should be seven important objects in the sky. And indeed there were seven objects that could be seen easily with the unaided eye: the planets Mercury, Venus,

Mars, Jupiter, and Saturn, and also the sun and moon. The seven days of our week are derived from these seven objects. The ancients believed that each of the seven objects was a god. They could not worship all the gods at the same time—and so they set aside a day for each one of them. Sunday was the day for worshiping the sun; Monday was the day for the moon; Tuesday was devoted to Mars. On the fourth day Mercury was worshiped; on the fifth day Jupiter; Friday was the day for paying homage to Venus; and Saturday was Saturn's day. Now that all the gods had been appeased, the ancients were back to the sun's day once more.

For hundreds of years people were content with this limited view of the universe. But there were men who were not willing to accept the mystical number seven. They believed there were important objects in the skies in addition to those basic seven. In 1610 their beliefs were strengthened—for in that year Galileo looked into the sky through the telescope, recently invented by Hans Lippershey, the Dutch lens maker. Galileo discovered four of Jupiter's satellites. During the years between 1610 and 1684 five satellites of Saturn were discovered.

Almost a hundred years passed by before the discovery of the sixth planet. Very likely no astronomer even dreamed of the addition of another planet to the five already known.

William Herschel, a German musician who in later life became an astronomer and a naturalized citizen of England, studied the heavens carefully and became thoroughly familiar with the sky. He knew the way it should appear. One evening as he looked into the sky, he noticed a strange object among the stars. He thought the object was a comet and told the Astronomer Royal about it. The king's astronomer observed the object but did not agree that it was a comet.

Several months later other astronomers viewed the object.

They made many observations and then figured mathematically that the object was indeed a planet. They determined that the planet was twice as far from the sun as Saturn, and that it would go around the sun once in 84 years. Later it was found that at least twenty other astronomers had seen this strange object among the stars. But not a single one of them was aware that the object was a planet.

Herschel called the new planet George's Star, after King George III. Other astronomers called the object Herschel's planet. But neither of those names persisted. Bode suggested that the new planet should be named after Uranus, the god of ancient mythology who represented Heaven and was the husband of Earth.

Some people have said that Herschel's discovery of Uranus was an accident. It is true that Herschel was not looking for a planet when he studied the skies almost 200 years ago, and from that standpoint the discovery was an accident. But if Herschel had not known the skies, if he had not been curious, his sighting of the object would have gone unreported. Herschel knew what to do with his observation, which makes it more important than something he just happened to stumble onto. Herschel himself wrote this about the discovery: "It has generally been supposed that it was a lucky accident that brought this star into my view; this is an evident mistake. In the regular manner I examined every star of the heavens, and it was that night its turn to be discovered. . . . I perceived the visible planetary disk as soon as I looked at it."

The discovery of Uranus jogged men's thoughts. They had believed that they knew all about the system of planets that circled the sun. Now they had to change their ideas—and this was not an easy task.

Uranus is slow-moving; it takes 84 earth years for the planet to go around the sun. Since its discovery Uranus has gone around the sun only a little more than twice. In other words, only a little more than two Uranian years have passed. Although Uranus takes a long time to go around the sun, it spins very fast on its axis, completing a turn in 10 hours and 45 minutes. Days are very short indeed on Uranus—only about 6 hours from sunrise to sunset. Because Uranus is so far from the earth, we cannot be sure about the rotation period; it may be a half hour longer or shorter.

Many astronomers have observed faint bands or belts on this sea-green planet, similar to those observed on Jupiter. They have not seen distinct markings on the planet, of the kind that would enable more accurate measurement of the rotation period.

Like Jupiter and Saturn, Uranus has a dense, opaque atmosphere. And also like those two planets, the atmosphere of Uranus is probably made up of methane gas for the most part. Small amounts of ammonia have also been detected in the Uranian atmosphere. However, it is so cold there that most of the ammonia gas has been frozen into the solid form. The atmosphere, therefore, has considerably more methane in it than ammonia. Since Uranus is farther from the sun than Jupiter and Saturn, its temperature is lower, probably in the neighborhood of −300 degrees F.

The tilt of the axis of Uranus from the vertical to the plane of its orbit is very unusual. Our axis is tilted 23½ degrees from the vertical to the plane of our orbit around the sun. The axis of Uranus is tilted 98 degrees from the vertical to the plane of its orbit around the sun. This unusual situation results in strange effects. For example, during almost 21 earth years (one quarter of its revolution around the sun) all of the northern half of Uranus is in continuous darkness. The opposite half of the planet is in continuous daylight. Later on, the situation is reversed: the

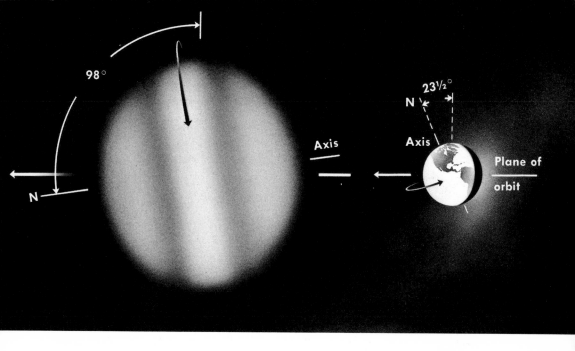

part of Uranus which was in darkness will then be in daylight, and the brightly lighted half will be in darkness.

The extreme tilt of the planet means that for several years we see mostly one of the polar regions of Uranus. Then, for about 20 years, we see the equatorial region; for another 20 years we see the other pole; then the equator; and so on. In 1945 a pole of

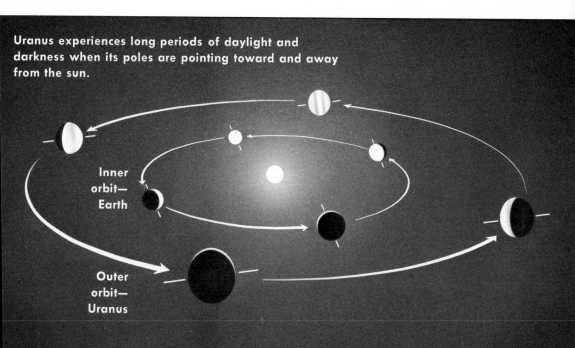

Uranus experiences long periods of daylight and darkness when its poles are pointing toward and away from the sun.

Inner orbit— Earth

Outer orbit— Uranus

the planet was about at the center of the disk as we saw it. In 1966 the equator was at the center of the image that we saw. If we could see Uranus clearly, its appearance would be quite strange. Sometimes it would look like a wheel turning about a central point; at other times it would appear as a spinning ball viewed from the side. Unfortunately we cannot usually see Uranus well enough to observe these strange appearances clearly.

Five small satellites, the largest only about 1000 miles in diameter, revolve around Uranus. Each of them is in the plane of the planet's equator.

Uranus can sometimes be seen with the unaided eye. It looks like a very dim star. Because it is so faint, we usually say that an observer needs a telescope to see Uranus—the seventh planet in order of distance from the sun. We suggest that you wait until you get a telescope to see Uranus in the nighttime sky; for you would need a very clear night, and also very good eyes, to see it otherwise.

NEPTUNE

diameter   27,700 miles

distance from the sun   2,791,000,000 miles

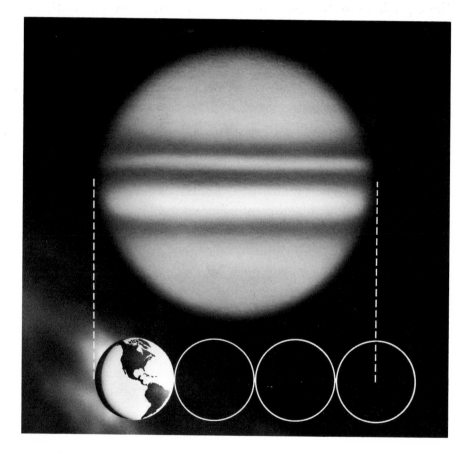

NEPTUNE WAS "DISCOVERED" BEFORE IT WAS SEEN. This is a curious statement, but it is a true one. How can you look into the heavens and be sure that an unknown planet is there, even though you cannot see it? Well, this is the way it was done.

After they have made a few observations of a particular planet, astronomers have enough information to calculate its orbit. They can do this with great accuracy. By completing equations and solving many mathematical problems, they know exactly where the planet will be at any time in the future. In order to make these predictions, the astronomer must consider the gravitational attraction of other planets that are close by.

After Uranus was discovered, astronomers calculated the orbit of the planet. For about 20 years Uranus behaved as it should: it arrived at a given point in its orbit at the precise time the astronomers expected it. But by about 1840 the planet was not at the place it should be. It was not far away, to be sure. However, even the slightest difference between the actual position and the predicted position is not allowable; there must be some explanation for the variation. Astronomers knew that planets change the motions of other objects nearby. Jupiter and Saturn were close by; but even when the effects of these planets were considered, Uranus still did not behave as it should.

The problem was interesting. Some people thought the variation of Uranus proved that the laws of gravitation do not apply at great distances. Others thought there must be a planet out beyond Uranus that was affecting its motion in orbit. John Couch Adams, a young English student, was one who believed this. In 1841 he determined to search for the new planet as soon as he was graduated from college. In 1843 he started on the search.

Adams spent several years working out mathematical problems to determine that there was another planet, and also to determine where it was located. In October 1845 he had a solution. Adams went to the Astronomer Royal, Sir George Airy, and asked him to search a certain section of the sky for the unknown planet.

But Airy was not at all convinced there was a planet. In fact he believed that the variations in the motion of Uranus resulted from other causes. Also, the part of the sky that Adams wanted him to search was not charted. It would take years to find a new planet. Airy laid the problem aside, and nothing further happened for almost eight months. Airy probably believed that discovering a planet was a task for men with considerable experience. Adams was just an upstart—a young man who had only recently been graduated from college.

In the meantime Leverrier, a French mathematician, independently attacked the same problem. In June 1846 he published a paper which gave the position where the new planet should be found. Airy read the paper and noticed that the location was just about the same as the one Adams had suggested eight months earlier. Now Airy was convinced that there was a new planet. He asked the Cambridge Observatory to look for it. Challis, the astronomer there, did not map his observations; and so, even though he looked at the new planet, he did not know it.

Leverrier had written to Galle, a German astronomer at the Berlin Observatory, requesting him to look for the unknown planet. On September 23, 1846, the same day that he received the letter, Galle and his assistant found the new planet.

Controversy raged over who should have credit for the discovery. Today we usually credit both Adams and Leverrier, for both men proved the reliability of mathematics: both of them "discovered" a planet before they saw it.

Arago, a Frenchman, suggested that the new planet be called Leverrier. But this suggestion was not well received outside France, and so Arago suggested that it be called Neptune.

Neptune is farther from the sun than Uranus, and so it is colder: about −350 degrees F. The ammonia that would be gaseous if the planet were warmer is frozen solid. Therefore the atmosphere that surrounds the planet is composed of methane gas. In a telescope Neptune appears blue-green. This is because the atmosphere absorbs most of the red part of the sunlight that falls on the planet and so reflects the blues and greens.

There would be a long, long time between birthdays if you lived on Neptune. It takes almost 165 years for the planet to go around the sun once—165 earth years equal 1 Neptune year. While it is going around the sun, Neptune spins on its axis once in about 16 hours. There are over 90,000 days in a single year on this planet.

Two satellites revolve around Neptune. Triton, the larger one, is about the size of the earth's moon. Nereid, the smaller one, is probably only 200 miles in diameter.

Neptune is a cold, distant world that we know very little about. The most important thing about the planet is the way it was discovered. It was a remarkable achievement of mathematics, for it showed the value of careful reasoning and of careful figuring that used the laws of mathematics.

PLUTO

diameter   3,600(?) miles

distance from the sun   3,664,000,000 miles

THE DISCOVERY OF NEPTUNE HELPED ASTRONOMERS COMPUTE THE
ORBIT OF URANUS. But further observations of Uranus and Neptune still did not agree with predictions. Many people believed
that there was another planet in addition to Neptune that was
exerting force on Uranus, causing it to move in a manner that
varied from the predictions.

During the early part of this century many astronomers studied
the problem. The most energetic investigator was Percival Lowell, who built an observatory at Flagstaff, Arizona, to study the
planets. Lowell worked steadily on the problem without solving
it before he died in 1916. Part of his failure was due to the kind
of telescope he had available: the instrument covered only a very
small area of the sky.

In 1929 Lowell's brother gave money to build a telescope that
could map large areas. It showed thousands of stars in a single
photograph. Now it was possible to picture a large part of the
sky at once; and so the work of exploring the heavens was
speeded up. Machines were invented to study the photographs
made by cameras attached to the new telescope.

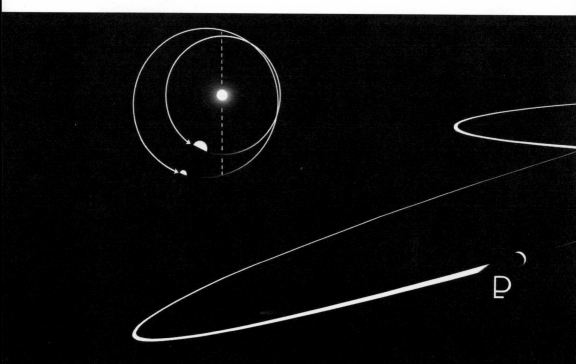

Early in 1930 Clyde W. Tombaugh, a young assistant at Lowell Observatory in Flagstaff, while studying these photos saw a faint object that he calculated must be a billion miles beyond Neptune. Observations made later showed that the object was changing position among the stars—and so proved it to be a member of the sun's family. The new planet was called Pluto. Its discovery was announced on March 13, 1930.

The orbit of this outermost planet is unusual. As the diagram shows, during most of its orbit Pluto is the most distant of all the planets; yet it is closer to us than Neptune during part of its orbit. It will be at its closest in 1989. Also, Pluto's orbit is more inclined to the earth's orbit plane (17 degrees) than is that of any of the other planets.

Pluto is so far away that it is impossible to obtain accurate information about it. For example, many attempts have been made to measure its diameter. An outstanding effort was made by Gerard P. Kuiper, a Dutch-American astronomer, who found the diameter to be 3600 miles. Many astronomers believe the diameter is larger—closer to that of earth, which is about 8000

Pluto is not always the most distant planet. In 1987 it will move in closer to the earth than Neptune.

miles. As a matter of record Kuiper did report a diameter of 6400 miles after a different study was completed. More studies need to be made before we can be sure about the size of Pluto. Tremendous difficulties must be overcome to make such astronomical observations. Astronomers must continually check their findings to be sure no error has been committed.

Pluto is so distant that powerful telescopes are needed to see it. Astronomers who observe the planet to gain knowledge of its detail must be extremely careful and patient. In 1955 two astronomers, Merle F. Walker and Robert Hardie of the Lowell Observatory, announced that they had discovered the rotation period of Pluto. They had studied the planet for several months, observing its changing brightness. This gave them a clue to the rotation period. They announced that Pluto takes 6 days and 9 hours to make a complete rotation.

Small bits of knowledge such as this are added to previous knowledge. Gradually, after years of hard work and after many men have made contributions, we are able to establish quite accurately the nature of these distant worlds.

Gerard Kuiper created considerable excitement early in 1956: he announced that his computations showed (as he had predicted in an article in 1953) that Pluto had been a satellite of Neptune at one time. He said that Pluto once moved around Neptune much as the moon moves around the earth. But Pluto escaped from Neptune's attraction and so became a planet—an object moving in a predictable orbit about the sun. Kuiper's explanation of the history of Pluto may or may not be entirely true. It is certainly true that at this time Pluto is a full-fledged planet.

The year on Pluto is long indeed—248 earth years. Earth people living on Pluto would never reach a ripe old age; in fact it would be most unusual to reach an age of ½ year.

We are not at all sure that Pluto has an atmosphere. If it does, the main part of it is probably methane. But maybe the methane is liquefied, so that there are great oceans of it; or perhaps it is frozen solid. Certainly the temperature on Pluto must be very low. Some have suggested it is as low as —400 degrees F.

Are there planets beyond Pluto? Many have wondered. Right now no one can say yes or no. There may be planets that belong to our system out beyond Pluto, billions of miles distant. On the other hand Pluto may be alone out there: the loneliest world in the solar system, cold, plunged in everlasting dim light—the frontier of the sun's planets.

Further Readings

Branley, Franklyn M. *The Earth: Planet Number Three.* New York: Thomas Y. Crowell Company, 1966.

————. *Mars: Planet Number Four.* New York: Thomas Y. Crowell Company, 1965.

————. *The Sun: Star Number One.* New York: Thomas Y. Crowell Company, 1964.

Gallant, Roy. *Exploring the Planets* (new ed.). Garden City, N.Y.: Doubleday & Company, Inc., 1967.

Moore, Patrick. *A Guide to the Planets.* New York: W. W. Norton & Company, Inc., 1954.

————. *Picture History of Astronomy.* Grosset & Dunlap, Inc., 1961.

Pickering, James S. *1001 Questions Answered about Astronomy.* New York: Dodd, Mead & Co., 1966.

Polgreen, John and Cathleen. *The Earth in Space.* New York: Random House, Inc., 1963.

Sagan, Carl, Jonathan Leonard and editors of Life Magazine. *Planets.* New York: Time Inc., 1966.

Simon, Tony. *The Search for Planet X.* New York: Basic Books, Inc., 1962.

Skilling, William T., and Robert S. Richardson. *Sun, Moon, and Stars.* New York: McGraw-Hill Book Company, Inc., 1948.

Wyler, Rose, and Gerald Ames. *The Golden Book of Astronomy.* New York: Simon and Schuster, Inc., 1955.

Index